MASTERPIECES OF RENAISSANCE ART

Eight Rediscoveries

MASTERPIECES OF RENAISSANCE ART
Eight Rediscoveries

By Andrew Butterfield and Anthony Radcliffe

With essays by Charles Avery
Alfredo Bellandi
Raffaele Casciaro
A. Victor Coonin
Giancarlo Gentilini

Salander-O'Reilly
NEW YORK

This catalogue accompanies an exhibition from
November 29, 2001 to February 2, 2002

Salander-O'Reilly Galleries, LLC

20 East 79 Street New York, NY 10021

Tel (212) 879–6606 Fax (212) 744–0655

www.salander.com

Gallery hours: Monday–Saturday 9:30 to 5:30

CONTENTS

FLORENTINE SCULPTURE

DESIDERIO DA SETTIGNANO

Cherub's Head

DESIDERIO DA SETTIGNANO
(Settignano c. 1429–Florence 1464)

CHERUB'S HEAD
Marble, 32 x 47 cm. (12 $^1/_2$ x 18 $^1/_2$ inches),
c. 1460–1464

Provenance:
Arthur Sambon, Paris
Carlo de Carlo, Florence

Bibliography:
*Collection Arthur Sambon, Catalogue des Objets
D'Art et de Haute Curiosité*, Galerie Georges Petit,
Paris, 25–28 May 1914, lot 404, illustrated.

I. Cardellini, *Desiderio da Settignano*, Milan, 1962,
pp.252–256, (illustrated fig. 316).

A. Markham, Review of *Desiderio da Settignano* by
I. Cardellini, *Art Bulletin*, LXVI, 2, 1964, p. 246.

U. Middeldorf, *Sculptures from the Samuel H. Kress
Collection, European Schools XIV–XIX Century*,
London, 1976, pp. 16–19.

fig. 1
Desiderio da Settignano,
Tabernacle of the Sacrament
(detail), San Lorenzo,
Florence

This relief features the head of a cherub framed by interlocking cornucopia and acanthus stalks tied together by a ribbon. There can be no doubt that the piece is by Desiderio da Settignano, who was responsible for some of the most celebrated relief sculpture of the Renaissance.

Knowledge of Desiderio's oeuvre rests primarily on two important documented commissions, both in Florence: the Monument of Carlo Marsuppini, in Santa Croce, and the Tabernacle of the Sacrament, in San Lorenzo. The work in Santa Croce was likely begun shortly after Marsuppini's death in 1453 and carried on at least through 1459. The monument displays foliage on the sarcophagus, fluttering ribbons on its base, and feathered wings at its corners similar to those features found on the present relief. Vasari especially praised its decorative elements: "Among other parts of the said work are seen certain wings… which seem to be made not of marble but of real feathers, difficult things to imitate in marble, seeing that the chisel is not able to counterfeit hair and feathers" (G. Vasari, *Lives of the Painters, Sculptors and Architects*, New York, 1996, p. 474). The same praise could be said of the present sculpture, which, like the Marsuppini monument is a work of virtuoso carving at the highest level of technical achievement.

Desiderio's tabernacle in San Lorenzo was completed in 1461. The *Cherub's Head* is manifestly similar to this sculpture and likely dates from the same period. The face of the present putto is similar to that of the male figure on the right in the tabernacle's Pietà relief (fig. 1) and the putto head on the left in the tabernacle's lunette (fig. 2). In particular, all three share the same broad face, open-mouthed expression and lightly tousled hair. Desiderio turns the faces toward the spectator's right in three-quarter view. The foreshortened perspective is most successful when seen directly in front. The other putti and angels that populate the tabernacle's central unit are likewise similar to the present relief in physiognomy and expression.

fig. 2
Desiderio da Settignano,
Tabernacle of the Sacrament
(detail), San Lorenzo,
Florence

In both the tabernacle and the present relief, the forms emerge as a series of planes carved parallel to the pictorial surface. This manner is wholly indicative of Desiderio, who typically emphasizes expressive nuance over plasticity; it is one of the hallmarks of his *schiacciato* reliefs. Thus the tabernacle figures exude an uncommon spiritual intensity and the face of the present putto pulses with animated excitement.

Desiderio typically adds to his works unexpected and delightful details based on life study. In the present relief these are seen in the double chin and fleshy neck of the child-like putto, the undulating tips of its softly feathered wings, and the wandering tendrils that emerge from the acanthus stalk decoration. Technical details also confirm Desiderio's authorship, especially the drill marks that the sculptor characteristically leaves evident as a distinctive flair. The drill holes seen in the present relief are especially evident at the sides of the putto's mouth, nose, and ear, and in the shadows around the edges of the acanthus leaves.

The *Cherub's Head* must originally have been part of an impressive decorative display of considerable importance. It has been hypothetically associated with the celebrated tabernacle that Desiderio executed for the church of San Pier Maggiore in Florence. The church was destroyed in 1784 and Desiderio's tabernacle dismantled at that time. Vasari gives a short account of the piece: "In San Piero Maggiore, also, he made the Tabernacle of the Sacrament in marble with his usual diligence; and although there are no figures on this work, yet it shows his beautiful manner and infinite grace, like his other works" (Vasari, *op.cit.*, p. 474). Something of its appearance is known from a lengthy description by Francesco Bocchi (*Le bellezze della città di fiorenza*, Florence, 1591, p. 175). Among other details, he specified that the tabernacle was an eight-sided structure resting on a multi-tiered base, and that the third tier of this base was decorated with cherubim: "nel terzo sono quattro cherubini." Presumably this section would have consisted of a cubic plinth that had

one cherub carved in relief, in a fashion similar to that of the *Cherub's Head*, on each of its four sides. Cardellini (1962, pp. 252–256) argued forcefully that the present relief could be the only surviving element from this tabernacle.

Cardellini also noted that the *Cherub's Head* has almost identical dimensions as the four reliefs of cherubs found on the base of a ciborium attributed to Desiderio in the National Gallery of Art in Washington. That ciborium too has been associated with the San Pier Maggiore tabernacle. But the structure in Washington is in fact a pastiche of elements (both fifteenth-century and later) and its form differs in significant ways from Bocchi's description, including the fact that it has six sides rather than eight. Moreover, the putti heads on its base are radically dissimilar from the style of Desiderio and cannot be by the master. Cardellini believed that these reliefs were modern forgeries derived from the present sculpture. However, both Markham (1964, p. 246) and Middeldorf (1976, p. 19 n.20) regarded the *Cherub's Head* as unrelated to the Washington structure. In any case, the *Cherub's Head* is far superior to any decorative element on the work in Washington. The present work may even be the only authentic surviving relief from Desiderio's famous tabernacle for San Pier Maggiore.

Nevertheless, it is possible that the *Cherub's Head* may have been made for another of the many types of decorative ensembles for which Desiderio was so well regarded. Desiderio created several significant works of architectural ornament that are documented but now lost. These include the base for Donatello's bronze *David*, which stood in the courtyard of the Palazzo Medici, two water basins and one chimneypiece commissioned through the art dealer Bartolomeo Serragli, and windows above the loggia of a home owned by the Ghiberti family at San Giuliano a Settimo. Extant examples of decorative ornament from Desiderio's studio include the Boni Chimneypiece, in the Victoria and Albert Museum in London, and the Boni coat of arms, in the Detroit Institute of Arts. These examples, however, are carved in *pietro di macigno* sandstone and Desiderio is known to have specialized in marble.

A. Victor Coonin

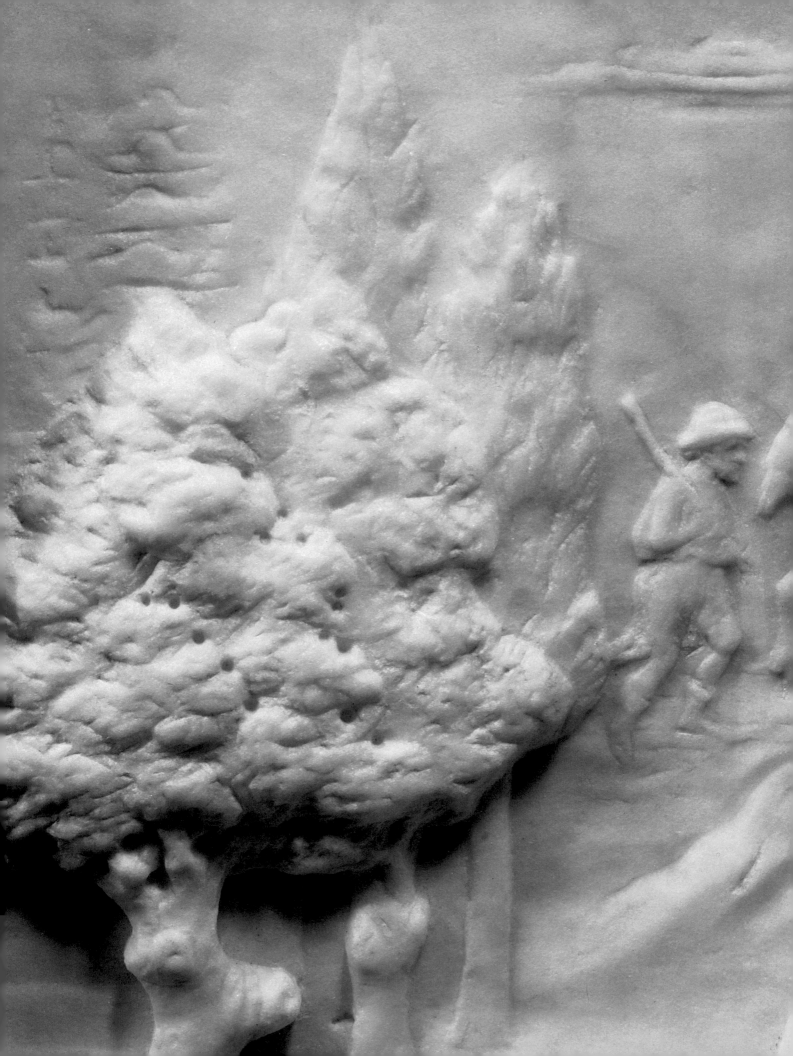

ANTONIO ROSSELLINO

St. Jerome in the Wilderness

ANTONIO ROSSELLINO
(Settignano c. 1427– c. 1479 Florence)

ST. JEROME IN THE WILDERNESS
Marble, 42.6 x 38 cm. (16 $^3/_4$ x 15 inches),
c. 1470–1475

Provenance:

Stefano Bardini, Florence

Luigi Bellini, Florence

Carlo de Carlo, Florence

Bibliography:

The Beautiful Art Treasures and Antiquities. The Property of Signor Stefano Bardini, American Art Galleries, New York, April 23–27, 1918, lot 420.

U. Procacci, *La casa Buonarotti a Firenze*, Milan, 1967, p. 198.

R. Wittkower, "Desiderio da Settignano's 'St. Jerome in the Desert'" in *Idea and Image*, London, 1978, pp. 145–46.

G. Gentilini, *I Della Robbia*, Florence, 1992, p. 361.

A. Bellandi in G. Gentilini, *I Della Robbia e l'"arte nuova" della scultura invetriata*, catalogue of an exhibition at Basilica di Sant' Alessandro Fiesole, Florence, 1998, pp. 291–292.

M. Scalini, "Antonio Rossellino, San Gerolamo in penintenza," in M. Scalini and A. Tartuferi, eds., *Un tesoro rivelato. Capolavori dalla Collezione Carlo de Carlo*, catalogue of an exhibition at the Galleria dell'Academia, Florence, March, 2001, p. 57, and color plate XV.

fig. 1
Antonio Rossellino,
Adoration of the Shepherds,
Museo Nazionale del
Bargello, Florence

Until it was exhibited at the Accademia in Florence in March of this year, the present relief had not been seen in public since the Stefano Bardini sale in New York in 1918. As a result of this long absence, the sculpture has never received the attention its beauty and significance would otherwise have elicited. It is among the most remarkable relief sculptures of the early Renaissance. The entire surface seems to flicker with light, creating an extraordinary sense of animate vitality. The animals all appear to be in motion, and the clouds and trees seem to move gently in the breeze. More exceptional still is the intensity of St. Jerome's expression: he exhibits an almost desperate yearning for spiritual comfort and release. The spatial illusion of the sculpture is another noteworthy aspect. It is calculated with enormous sophistication, and it it is no exaggeration to observe that the piece is one of the great masterpieces of pictorial relief from the Renaissance.

Both in the catalogue of the Bardini sale and in the catalogue of the recent exhibition in Florence, the relief was ascribed to Antonio Rossellino. The evidence to support this attribution is abundant and definitive. For example, the landscape is exactly comparable in treatment with the landscapes in two famous reliefs by the artist, a tondo of the *Adoration of the Shepherds* (Museo Nazionale del Bargello, Florence; fig. 1), and an altarpiece of the same subject in Sant'Anna dei Lombardi, Naples (fig. 2). In all three works, the rockery soars upward in an arc that rises above the heads of the figures, filling the background of the relief. In all three reliefs the surface of the rockery is made irregular by a series of long vertical grooves or depressions with flickering outlines. Moreover, the treatment of flora and vegetation is nearly identical. The scrub, fern and thistle scattered in the foreground of the present relief are the same in form and treatment as the plants in the foreground of the relief in Naples (fig. 3). An identical thistle plant also appears in the foreground of Antonio Rossellino's relief of the *Ascension* of the Virgin on the Prato Pulpit.

fig. 2
Antonio Rossellino,
Adoration of the Shepherds,
Sant'Anna dei Lombardi,
Naples

The trees as well are highly similar. In the present sculpture, the trees in the middle ground at the side edges of the relief have trunks that zig-zag upward between a series of stumps. A tree with the same kind of trunk appears in the middle distance of the Naples relief, immediately to the left of the seated shepherd; the posts of the manger in the Bargello tondo are also covered with stumps of comparable shape. The cypresses in the background of the present sculpture, too, are highly like the cypresses in the distance in the Naples relief. The clouds in the present sculpture resemble the clouds both in the Naples relief and in the frame of the Bargello tondo.

Another indication of Rossellino's authorship is the exquisite representation of animal life. The dragon in the lower right corner of the sculpture is highly similar in form with the beast in a relief of Hercules and the Hydra, in Sant'Anna dei Lombardi (fig. 4). They share virtually identical heads, wings, long articulated necks, and furry paws. The physiognomy of the dragon also closely resembles that of the dragons by Antonio Rossellino on the *lavamano* in the Old Sacristy of San Lorenzo. (On the attribution of the *lavamano* to Rossellino, see A. Butterfield, *The Sculptures of Andrea del Verrocchio*, New Haven and London, 1997, pp. 10–12.) The beautiful stag at the right in the present sculpture can be compared with the sheep immediately behind the dog in the Naples relief. Not only do they both have compact ovoid bodies, they even stand with their legs in exactly the same pose.

fig. 3
Antonio Rossellino,
Adoration of the Shepherds
(detail), Sant'Anna dei
Lombardi, Naples

Given the strength of the evidence, it is no wonder that the attribution to Antonio Rossellino has been accepted by a wide range of scholars, including Anthony Radcliffe, Giancarlo Gentilini, Antonio Paolucci, Franca Falletti, Mario Scalini and Alfredo Bellandi. (Rudolf Wittkower, who knew the relief only in photograph, also tentatively accepted the attribution.) To judge from the many points of similarity, the present sculpture was almost certainly carved in the same period as the Naples relief, c. 1475.

The sculpture seems to have achieved a measure of fame during the Renaissance. At least three copies of it survive, in glazed terracotta, attributable to Luca della Robbia il Giovane. One is in the Museo di Casa Buonarotti, Florence, and one is in the Victoria and Albert Museum; a third was last recorded in the Bardini sale in 1918. (J. Pope-Hennessy, *Catalogue of the Italian Sculpture in the Victoria and Albert Museum*, London, 1964, p. 256; and A.Bellandi, 1998, pp. 291–292.).

It is possible that the present sculpture was in the Palazzo della Signoria in the sixteenth century. "Un quadro di marmo di basso rilievo d'un S. Girolamo" is recorded in the 1553 inventory of the Palazzo (see C. Conti, *La prima reggia di Cosimo I de' Medici*, Florence, 1893, p. 141). Cardellini suggested that this document might refer to Desiderio's relief of the same subject, now in the National Gallery of Art, Washington (see I. Cardellini, *Desiderio da Firenze*, Milan, 1962, p. 244). But according to Rudolf Wittkower (1978, p. 245), this connection is "wishful thinking"; and the document could refer just as well to Rossellino's marble. Indeed, Rossellino's relief was copied in the sixteenth century, but Desiderio's was not. From this one might infer that Rossellino's relief was better known (and in a more public location) than Desiderio's was in the sixteenth century. Moreover, as Anthony Radcliffe has pointed out to me, Vasari in 1550 in *On Technique* makes a clear distinction between "basso rilievo" and "stiacciato rilievo" (i.e. low relief

fig. 4
Antonio Rossellino, *Hercules and the Hydra*, Sant'Anna dei Lombardi, Naples

and flattened relief). The Rossellino is a "basso rilievo," whereas the Desiderio is a "stiacciato rilievo." It thus seems that Rossellino corresponds better to the relief recorded in the Palazzo.

In the 1553 inventory, the marble is listed among the contents of the "Prima stanza della Guardaroba segreta." This room served as a kind of treasury for the Medici family. Its contents included nineteen portraits of the Medici and works by Titian, Leonardo, Michelangelo, Desiderio da Settignano, Donatello, Bronzino and Tribolo. There can be little doubt that the marble relief of St. Jerome in the room was likewise a highly regarded possession of Cosimo I de' Medici.

St. Jerome's *Letters* give a vivid description of his physical and spiritual hardship as an ascetic and hermit in the desert. For example, in Letter XXII he says: "My unkempt limbs were covered in shapeless sackcloth… my face was pale with fasting… When all other help failed me, I used to fling myself at Jesus's feet; I watered them with my tears, I wiped them with my hair… I remember that often I joined night to day with my wailings and ceased not from beating my breast till tranquility returned to me at the Lord's behest… I would make my way alone into the desert; and when I came upon some hollow valley or rough mountain or precipitous spot, there I would set up my oratory, and make that spot a place of torture for my unhappy flesh" (*Select Letters of St. Jerome*, trans F. A. Wright, Cambridge, Mass, 1933, pp. 67–69). Many of the elements in the present relief were taken directly from this letter.

Another important source for the iconography of the relief was the *Golden Legend*, a popular compendium of saints' lives. There one reads of how St. Jerome befriended a lion; how this lion, at Jerome's request, worked with a donkey to carry wood for Jerome's monastery; and how the donkey was stolen by some merchants passing by with their camels. This text helps to explain

both the lions in the foreground of the relief, and the camel and figure in the background.

Jerome's gaze seems to include not only the cross and the skull at its base, but also the stag beyond. The presence of the animal was perhaps meant to recall the famous passage from the *Song of Songs* (2:8–9) "Behold, he comes, leaping upon the mountains, bounding over the hills. My beloved is like a gazelle or a young stag." In medieval and Renaissance exegesis, these lines were widely interpreted as a reference to Christ.

A second possible interpretation of the symbolic meaning of the stag merits attention. Psalm 42 begins, "As a hart longs for flowing streams, so longs my soul for thee, O God. My soul thirsts for God, for the living God. When shall I come and behold the face of God? My tears have been my food day and night, while men say to me continually 'Where is your God?'" The imagery in Jerome's Letter XXII is reminiscent of that in the Psalm, and thus the stag is perhaps a symbol of the soul's desire for God.

In the present sculpture, St. Jerome appears as gaunt and beardless, with a large cranium, and a scrawny neck in which the tendons are especially prominent. This head type was common in Florentine paintings of St. Jerome around 1470–1480. Some important parallels are a painting of St. Jerome that is sometimes attributed to Verrocchio (Palazzo Pitti, Florence), an anonymous fresco fragment in San Domenico, Pistoia; and Leonardo's panel of *St. Jerome in the Desert* (Pinacoteca, Vatican City).

Vasari reports that Antonio Rossellino's works "have been much esteemed by Michelangelo and by all the rest of the supremely excellent artists" (G. Vasari, *Lives of the Painters, Sculptors and Architects*, New York, 1996, p. 469). In his assessment of Rossellino's place in the history of art, Vasari was unstinting in praise, ranking him second after Donatello among early Renaissance sculptors:

> He deserves fame and honor as a most illustrious example from which modern sculptors have
> been able to learn how those sculptures should be made that are to secure the greatest praise
> and fame by reason of their difficulties. For after Donatello he did most towards adding a
> certain finish and refinement to the art of sculpture, seeking to give such depth and round-
> ness to his figures that they appear wholly round and finished, a quality which had not been
> seen to such perfection in sculpture up to that time; and since he first introduced it, in the
> ages after his and in our own it appears a marvel (G. Vasari, *ibid.*, pp. 472–473).

Andrew Butterfield

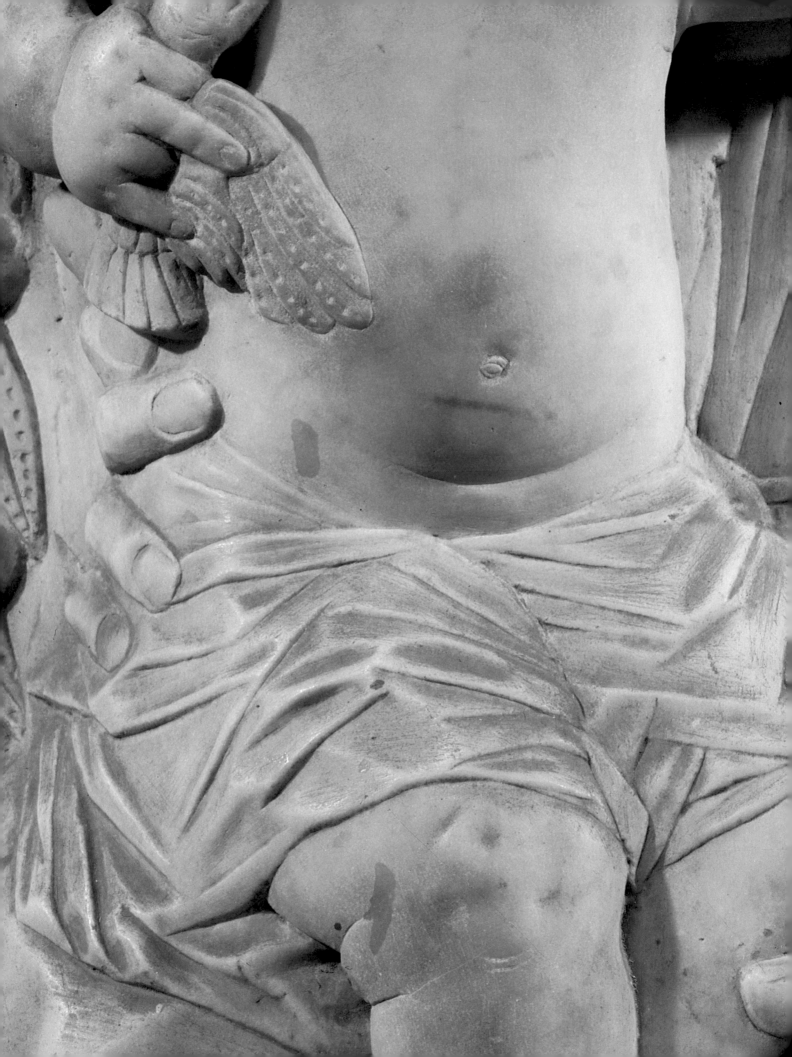

MASTER OF THE MARBLE MADONNAS

Madonna and Child

MASTER OF THE MARBLE MADONNAS
(active c. 1470–1500)

MADONNA AND CHILD ("THE CARUSO MADONNA")
marble, 81.5 x 56.5 cm. (31 $^3/_4$ x 22 $^1/_4$ inches),
c. 1470–1480

Provenance:
Guidi Family, Faenza
Galleria Sangiorgi, Rome
Enrico Caruso, New York
By descent to the previous owner

Bibliography:
S. Rubistein, "A Relief of the Quattrocento by the Master of the Marble Madonnas," *Art in America*, VII, 1919, pp. 104–110.

P. Key, *Enrico Caruso, A Biography*, Boston, 1922, pp. xiv, 249 (illustration facing p. 247)

J. Balogh, *Die Anfänge der Renaissance in Ungarn*, Graz, 1975, p. 181.

A. Bellandi, *Per un catalogo del Maestro delle Madonne in Marmo*, tesi di Specializzazione, Università degli Studi di Bologna, 1998, p. 19, I. 30.

It was Wilhelm von Bode at the end of the nineteenth century who first reconstructed the oeuvre of this artist and gave him the name the Master of the Marble Madonnas. As the sobriquet suggests, the artist is best known for reliefs of the Madonna; most of these are in marble, although examples in terracotta and stucco are also known. The works are characterized by a highly individual sense of form, relief and decorative motif. Trained in Florence, the Master also worked at the court of Urbino, in Emilia-Romagna, and for the King of Hungary. Ulrich Middeldorf has judged the Master of the Marble Madonnas "an artist of uncommon ability and inspiration" (U. Middeldorf, "Un Ecce Homo del Maestro delle Madonne di Marmo," *Arte Illustrata*, 57, 1974, pp. 2–9).

The works of Antonio Rossellino, such as the *Madonna dei Candelabri* (Salander-O'Reilly Galleries, New York), constitute the principal point of departure for the Master of the Marble Madonnas, and attest to his formation in Florence in the orbit of the great sculptors of the second half of the fifteenth century—not only Rossellino, but Mino da Fiesole and Benedetto da Maiano as well. His career parallels that of two other artists, who like the Master, were often active in regions outside of Florence: Domenico Rosselli (1439–1497/8) and Francesco di Simone Ferrucci (1437–1493), under whose influence perhaps, the Master carved the *Madonna* of the Via Capponi in Florence. In comparison with the sweet profiles and soft drapery of the Marian images of Rossellino, the Master displays a distinct personality. His reliefs tend toward an accentuated graphic stylization in the lines of the face, and in the sharp and squared-off folds of the drapery. The decorative elements, which show the influence of Mino da Fiesole, also share these characteristics. Another unmistakable feature is the tendency toward the flattening of some details, especially the hands of the Madonna. Adolfo Venturi has characterized the artist as "the idiosyncratic sculptor who make his angels laugh and who gives the Bambino the nose of a pussycat" (A. Venturi, *Storia dell'arte italiana*, Milan, 1908, pp. 660–70).

In the present work, the regal Madonna, crowned by two angels flying in mid-air on irregular clouds, sits enthroned. The Christ Child rests on her right leg; in His right hand, he holds a goldfinch, its mouth open; with His left hand he makes a gesture of blessing. The work is especially similar to four other reliefs that were carved in the same period (c. 1470–1480), but which show the Child on the Madonna's left leg, and which have candelabra in place of the garlands at the sides. These four are in 1) Museo Nazionale del Bargello, Florence, 2) the Metropolitan Museum of Art, 3) the National Gallery of Ottawa, where the version has a garland, similar in form to that in the present relief, but in a horizontal position, and 4) the National Gallery of Australia in Canberra (ex Daniel Katz Gallery; see *Daniel Katz Ltd. 1968–1993*, London, 1992, p. 12). There is also a related gesso cast in the Gipsoteca dell'Istituto Statale d' Arte di Firenze (C. Calloud, in *Donatello e il primo Rinascimento nei calchi della Gipsoteca*, Florence, 1985, pp. 202–203, no. 196), which was possibly made from the present relief sometime at the end of the nineteenth century, when the cast appeared in the catalogue of Manifattura Lelli. The cast testifies to the likelihood of the marble's Florentine provenance, and also shows that the piece enjoyed a certain success at the turn of the century.

The oldest record of the provenance of our relief is, as Stella Rubinstein noted (1919), at the beginning of the twentieth century, when the marble appeared in the catalogue of Galleria Sangiorgi, Rome (1902). Shortly later it was in the prestigious collection of the celebrated opera singer, Enrico Caruso. (Caruso began collecting seriously in 1906 in part to decorate his Villa Bellosguardo in Lastra a Signa, near Florence.) According to its credit line, the illustration of the relief in the 1922 biography of Caruso by Pierre Key was made in New York, and thus the relief must have been there after it was in Rome and before its return to Italy.

The sculpture is unusual among the Marian reliefs of the artist in that it has two *stemmi* or coats-of-arm. At the lower right, is a shield with a star, heart and cross, and two characters, possibly either a backward S and a P or the Greek letters *sigma* and *rho*. It is likely this *stemma* is for a confraternity or another religious institution. At the lower left is a shield with a bend dexter and three eight-pointed stars. This can possibly be identified as the coat-of-arms of the Ginori, the Florentine noble family. Thus, they seem to have been the original patrons of the sculpture.

Looking at works such as the present *Madonna and Child*, one regrets that the Master of the Madonnas traversed the panorama of late Quattrocento sculpture without leaving a clear indication of his identity. He is a significant but anonymous personality, and the attempts made so far to identify him have not been successful. Some scholars have tried to show that he is either Tommaso Fiamberti (1498–1524/5) or Giovanni Ricci (c. 1440–1523), the two Lombard sculptors responsible for the Numai Monument (1502) in Santa Maria dei Servi in Forlì. But these artists were in fact assistants to the Master of the Marble Madonnas, at least from the beginning of the early 1490s, as a tabernacle from 1491 shows. This tabernacle, which was formerly in Hreljin—a town in Croatia south of Fiume (see Balogh in *Matthias Corvinus und die Renaissance in Ungarn 1458–1542*, Vienna, 1982, p. 387)—forms a direct link with their other works in Romagna, which constitute a pale reflection of the Master of the Marble Madonnas (see Viroli, in *Melozzo da Forlì. La città e il suo tempo*, Forlì, 1994, p. 285, 299, 318–19).

I would like to consider another possibility of his identity, first suggested to me by Giancarlo Gentilini. In Casa Romei (Ferrara), there are two notable reliefs of the Roman emperors Marcus Aurelius and Antoninus Pius. Made in 1472, the reliefs are by the little known Florentine sculptor Gregorio di Lorenzo. Together with another ten reliefs, now lost, they formed a series of the Twelve Caesars that decorated the loggia of the Palazzo Ducale, erected by Ercole I d' Este. The comparison of the *Marcus Aurelius* with a relief of a *Roman Emperor* by the Master of the Marble Madonnas (Private Collection, Turin; see Ballandi, 1998, p. 26, I. 81 a, b) shows evident points of similarity throughout the sculpture, even in the way the decorative elements of the costume

have been carved. Still more revealing is the comparison of *Antoninus Pius* in Casa Romei with the Master's busts of the *Savior* at the Heim Gallery and Douai (for these, see Middeldorf 1974). Such correspondences suggest that Gregorio di Lorenzo may be the real identity of the Master of the Marble Madonnas. Indeed, if we did not know the name of the artist, we would attribute the reliefs in Ferrara to the Master of the Marble Madonnas.

Florence, Urbino and the cities in Hungary of Esztergom, Viségrad and Veszprém, where the Master worked in the 1480s for the court of Matthias Corvinus, were the principal centers for this itinerant sculptor. They bear witness to his role in the expansion of the visual culture of the Renaissance into Central Italy and transalpine Europe.

Alfredo Bellandi

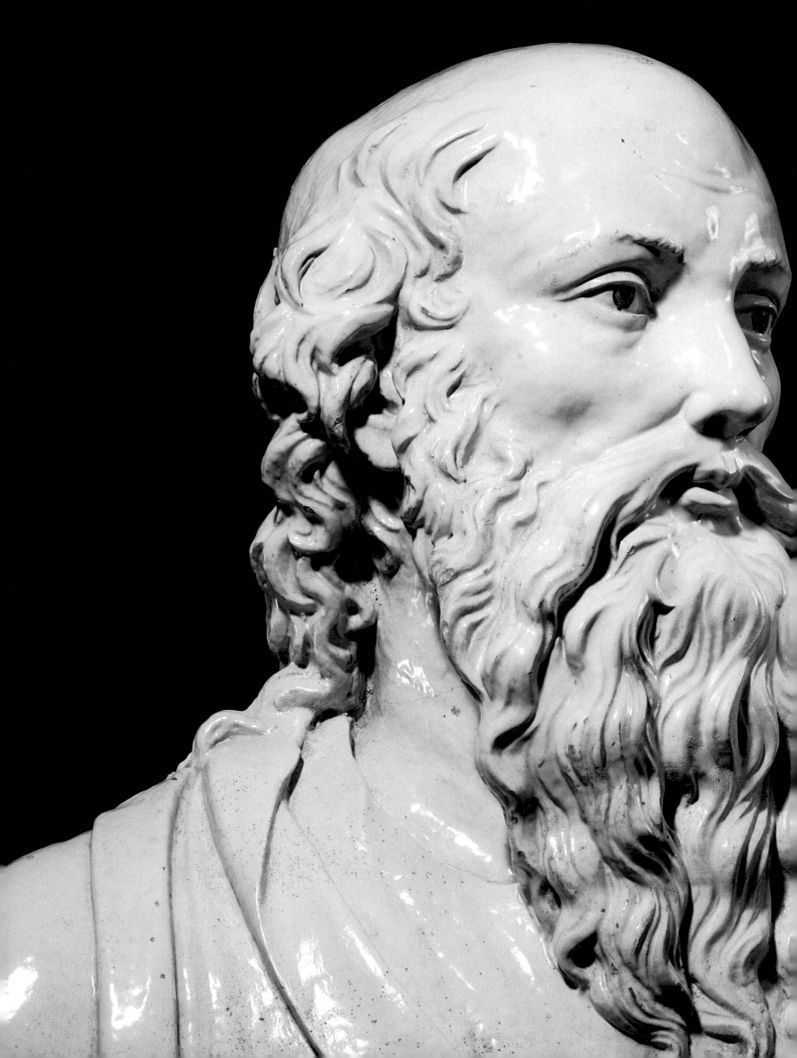

ANDREA DELLA ROBBIA

Apostle

ANDREA DELLA ROBBIA
(Florence, 1435–1525)

APOSTLE
Glazed terracotta, 43.5 x 54.5 cm. (17 x 21$^1/_2$ inches),
c. 1490

Provenance:
Émile Gavet, Paris
Private Collection, France

Bibliography:
*Catalogue des objets d'art et de haute curiosité de la
Renaissance, tableaux, tapisseries composant la
Collection de M. Émile Gavet*, Galerie Georges Petit,
Paris, 31 May–9 June 1897, p. 57, lot 190, pl. 190.

A. Marquand, *Andrea della Robbia and his Atelier*,
Princeton, 1922, I, p. 39, n. 26, fig. 34.

G. Gentilini, *I Della Robbia. La scultura invetriata
nel Rinascimento*, Firenze, 1992, p. 260.

G. Gentilini, in *Il Museo Bandini a Fiesole*, ed. by
M. Scudieri, Firenze 1993, p. 166.

A. Sigillo, in G. Gentilini, *I Della Robbia e l'«arte
nuova» della scultura invetriata*, catalogue of an exhibition held in Fiesole, May–November 1998,
Florence, 1998, pp. 210–211, fig. p. 210.

fig. 1
Andrea della Robbia,
St. Mark
Santa Maria delle Carceri,
Prato

This noble bust of a bearded man dressed in classical drapery does not have a distinguishing attribute and it is therefore difficult to be sure of his identity. Thoughtful, wise and solemn as a philosopher, but with an air of serene empathy and humanity, he probably is one of the Apostles. His long flowing beard and bald pate suggest that he might be St. Paul, St. Bartholomew, St. Andrew or St. John the Evangelist, who were often represented in this fashion by the Della Robbia (although in their oeuvre these figures are not always bald). His features are especially similar to those of St. Mark in a relief in Santa Maria della Carceri, Prato (fig. 1).

Until now this work was known only through a photograph in the 1897 catalogue of an auction in Paris of the collection of Emile Gavet; his collection was especially renowned for decorative arts and Renaissance terracottas. In that catalogue the work was attributed to Luca della Robbia and the figure was identified as St. Paul. In 1922, however, Allan Marquand ascribed the sculpture to Andrea della Robbia, Luca's nephew and artistic heir, on the basis of its affinities with a half-length figure of St. Bartholomew on the altar of Vieri Canigiani in Santa Croce, Florence. Marquand suggested that the bust likewise represented St. Bartholomew, and proposed a date for it in the 1470s.

Certainly, the palpable but measured naturalism, the sympathetic but reserved expression, and the brilliant but careful modeling fully confirm the attribution, as does the use of yellow in the irises of the eyes, a typical characteristic in works by Andrea. As already suggested elsewhere (Gentilini 1992 and 1993, Sigillo 1998), further proof of its authorship is found in comparison with two other busts that indubitably come from the same series. One of these works (42.5 x 56 cm.), now in a private collection in Florence, is a bust of a mature man with a short curly beard

fig. 2
Andrea della Robbia, *Apostle*
Private Collection, Florence

and preoccupied expression; he is perhaps St. Matthew (fig. 2). The other (43 x 54.5 cm.) formerly in the Campana collection, and since 1862 in the Musée du Louvre, is a bust of a beardless youth with thick, windswept hair, perhaps St. John (fig. 3).

The complex and animated modelling of the hair in all three works, as well as the emphatically plastic form of the drapery of the Louvre bust, indicate a date later than the one proposed by Marquand. On the basis of comparison with works such as the Evangelists in Santa Maria delle Carceri in Prato from 1491 (e.g. fig. 1), the present sculpture should be dated to the early 1490s, the moment of greatest artistic vivacity and originality in the mature period of Andrea della Robbia's career.

The hypothesis that the three busts belonged to the same group was initially based on their manifest similarities in iconography, typology (such as the unusual reduced development of the chest) and dimensions (Gentilini 1992). It is now possible to confirm the validity of this thesis due to direct examination of the three busts, two of which were included in the Della Robbia exhibition held in Fiesole in 1998 (Gentilini). Not only are the busts exactly alike in style, they also have the same facture and technique. All three statues were modeled in high relief, but with the back entirely open and carefully excavated, which is unusual in a bust. Moreover, all three busts manifest similar small imperfections in the enamel glaze on the terracotta (the smalt is less fluid and homogenous and more porous than is ideal). Finally, in all three busts along the rim of the back of the sculpture there is a border of unglazed terracotta about 4 cm. in dimension.

This shows that the busts were originally set in an architectural background, which was probably also made of glazed terracotta, molded and fired in sections, and painted either in ultramarine or another color in imitation of pietre dure. Most likely, this consisted of a series of lunette niches. Niches of this type are common in Andrea della Robbia's work; for example, they appear

fig. 3
Andrea della Robbia, *Apostle*
Museé du Louvre, Paris

in numerous eucharistic tabernacles where the white bust of Christ stands out against a blue niche (e.g. San Pietro, Anchiano, c. 1490–95; San Romolo, Tignano, 1494; Santi Jacopo e Filippo, Certaldo, 1503). Moreover, a comparable solution was frequently adopted by Andrea della Robbia in these years for similar *all'antica* busts which were set in roundels and frequently grouped in large ensembles. Those busts, too, often represent the Apostles (e.g. the so-called Sant'Ansano, in Museo Bandini, Fiesole). In our case, the high relief of the busts and measurements that such lunettes would have had to have had (approximately 50 x 100 cm.) suggest that they were displayed in separate lunettes, perhaps over doors (like the bust of Savior between adoring angels, today in the Palazzo Municipale of Borgo San Lorenzo) in the same architectural setting.

These three busts, therefore, are the sole remaining elements of a decorative enterprise of notable ambition and importance: most likely it included all twelve Apostles. It is worth emphasizing that, for the reasons of style already discussed, this series was made exactly in the years in which Andrea della Robbia and his workshop executed analogous series of busts *all'antica*, both of sacred and secular figures, for some of the most prestigious architectural settings in all Italy. These include the large medallions (perhaps eighteen or more) of the Aragonese Heroes for the Sala Grande of the Villa di Poggioreale in Naples (1492: the only surviving sculpture from this group is in the Museo di Capodimonte, Naples) and the series of Roman Emperors for the fortress of Castelnuovo di Testona in Piemontc (ca. 1490: only one surviving element today in the Museo Civico, Turin).

Giancarlo Gentilini

LUCA DELLA ROBBIA 'IL GIOVANE'

Adoring Angel

LUCA DELLA ROBBIA
'IL GIOVANE'
(Florence 1475–Paris 1548)

ADORING ANGEL
Partially glazed terracotta, 60 x 45 cm.
(23 ¹/₂ x 17 ¹/₂ inches), c. 1510–15

Provenance:
Carlo de Carlo, Florence

Bibliography:
G. Gentilini, *I Della Robbia. La scultura invetriata nel Rinascimento*, Florence, 1992, p. 332, illustrated in color on p. 347.

A. Radcliffe, "Two Adoring Angels, Workshop of Andrea della Robbia, c. 1510," in *The Thyssen-Bornemisza Collection. Renaissance and Later Sculpture*, London, 1992, pp. 100–105

A. Bellandi, "Luca della Robbia, detto Luca 'il Giovane'," in G. Gentilini, *I Della Robbia e l'«arte nuova» della scultura invetriata*, catalogue of an exhibtion held at Fiesole 29 May–1 November 1998, Florence, 1998, p. 283.

F. Petrucci, "Luca della Robbia 'Il Giovane' (?), Coppia di Putti reggifestone," in G. Gentilini, *I Della Robbia e l'«arte nuova» della scultura invetriata*, catalogue of an exhibtion held at Fiesole 29 May–1 November 1998, Florence, 1998, p. 301.

This relief represents an extraordinarily beautiful young Angel dressed in deacon vests, his features emphasized by the thick curls that fall in wavy locks down to his shoulders. He is shown in adoration—his hands are crossed on his chest in a gesture of humility—and his deeply moving expression conveys his love and anxious care. Modeled in high relief, the piece was realized with great technical skill, typical of the best works by the Della Robbia. The clay of the terracotta is light and strong; the back has been carefully excavated; and the colored glazing, which highlights parts of the vestments, is delicate in tonalilty. The glazed areas are intermixed with other unglazed areas, such as the skin, hair and sleeves, which were originally painted only after firing. (The sleeves still bear extensive traces of the original reddish pigment.) The practice of combining glazed and unglazed areas was adopted by Andrea della Robbia at the end of the Quattrocento in order to give his works greater naturalism in response to the demands of popular religion: indeed, one should recall that the Della Robbia were fervent followers of Savanarola.

The sculpture was acquired around 1990 by the celebrated Florentine collector and dealer, Carlo de Carlo. It is substantially integral, although it originally came from a work of much larger dimensions, that was made up from numerous pieces sectioned in a manner to hide their joins, then baked separately and rejoined *in situ*. This technique of manufacture was typical of the Della Robbia; it facilitated both the production of sculptures and their transportation, even over very long distances.

To clarify the original function and destination of the statue, one can compare it with an extremely similar pair of adoring Angels, which were sold in 1894 by Stefano Bardini to the Prince of Liechtenstein, and which today are in the Thyssen-Bornemisza Collection (Radcliffe 1992) These are so extraordinarily close to the present sculpture in style, typology, dimensions, technique and color that they must be considered parts of the same complex. The two Thyssen Angels still preserve the lower part of the figure down to the knees; and this termination plus the gentle arcing forward of the bodies shows that the figures originally were set in a lunette. Moreover, as observed by Anthony Radcliffe, the pronounced projection and noteworthy height of the figures (95.7 cm and 99.7 cm) makes it clear that they must have been in a lunette of unusual and impressive dimensions, presumably one over a large doorway or portal. A point of comparison is the Madonna and Child with Angels in the lunette over the central door of the cathedral of Pistoia. This group, made by Andrea with the help of Luca il Giovane della Robbia in 1504–05, measures 160 x 220 cm.

Given the discovery of the present work, we are now able to clarify that in this case there must have been at least two lunettes. This recalls the series executed by Andrea in 1507–8 for the façade by Giuliano Sangallo of the important Dominican convent of Santa Maria della Quercia in Viterbo, where the lunettes over the two lateral portals contain Dominican saints flanked by similar pairs of adoring Angels. Measuring 82 x 162 cm. those lunettes are in fact smaller than the

fig. 1
Luca della Robbia il
Giovane, *Angel*
Thyssen Collection, Madrid

ones that must have originally housed the present work and the Thyssen Angels. Therefore it is likely that our angels came from an edifice even greater in size where, because of the partial use of unglazed polychromy, the sculptures were set in a location at least partially protected from the rain (such as a portico or retrofacade).

At Viterbo the Angels in the lunette over the left portal have their hands joined in a prayerful gesture, exactly like the Thyssen Angels, while in the lunette over the right door, the hands are crossed over the chest, as in the present work. This fact permits us to imagine it paired with another angel in a similar pose. However, it is also possible that the gestures alternated with one another, as often happens in other lunettes by Andrea della Robbia. In that case, the present sculpture would have been paired with the Angel facing to the left with joined hands in the Thyssen Collection. It is more difficult to determine what were the central figures of the two lunettes, although one may have been, as astutely suggested by Anthony Radcliffe on the basis of various stylistic and material considerations, the monument statue of God the Father, preserved in fragmentary condition in the Victoria and Albert Museum in London. (That statue was acquired in Florence in 1859.)

fig. 2
Luca della Robbia il
Giovane, *Angel*
Thyssen Collection, Madrid

Based on their technique, typology, and iconography, the three Angels find many points of comparison with the work of the Della Robbia, especially in the bottega of Andrea around 1510. Radcliffe (1992) has already attributed the Thyssen angels, which were traditionally assigned to Giovanni della Robbia, to the bottega of Andrea, although he considered them to be "the work of assistants of varying degrees of sensitivity" (the left one is more vigorous and naturalistic, the right one is more timid and conventional). They are close to the angels supporting the curtain in the Tabernacle of the Sacrament in the church of Santi Apostoli in Florence. Andrea was paid for this work in 1512, and he executed it with the aid of assistants, perhaps including his sons Giovanni, Luca il Giovane and Girolamo.

On the other hand, if the vast production of the Della Robbia shop at the beginning of the Cinquecento often poses problems of precise attribution due to the collaboration of Andrea's five sons (as well as other assistants), we have clear evidence that the sons not only worked for their father, but also pursued independent projects both individually and together. In my opinion, many indications suggest that the present work and the Thyssen angels belonged to a project that was executed independently without the father. Indeed, in the works for which Andrea is responsible the vestments of the angels do not have sleeves which are gathered and puffed out above the elbows, as in the present work. Moreover, the use of partially glazed polychromy was rather rare in Andrea's oeuvre, and much more common in the works of his children, especially Luca il Giovane who seemed to prefer exactly the same palette of colors as is found in the present work.

Thus, as already has been proposed (Gentilini 1992, Bellandi 1998, Petrucci 1998) it is precisely to Luca il Giovane around 1510–15 that we should attribute the authorship of both this sculpture and the angels in the Thyssen Collection. These sculptures stand out among the later works of the Della Robbia, both for the touching and ineffable intensity of expression and for the delicate and varied modeling of the curly mane of hair. These features strongly reflect the influence of Leonardo. Moreover, the sculpture manifests a level of sensitivity, formal brilliance and cultural sophistication far superior to what is found in either the oeuvre of Giovanni or the late works of Andrea.

Biographical data about Luca il Giovane is scarce, and yet it suffices to show that he was an artist of exceptional talent and fame. Vasari informs us that Luca was "molto diligente negl'invetriati" and dedicated "alla scultura" and his documented works include a number of highly prestigious commissions. Chief among these are the pavement of the Logge in Vatican, ordered by Raphael (1518), the spectacular coat-of-arms of the Bartolini Salimbeni family, which is modeled with a refined virtuosity without parallel in the entire output of the Della Robbia family (1521; Museo del Bargello, Florence) and his celebrated work, made in conjunction with his brother Girolamo, for the court of Francis I. Around this core of documented works it is possible to reconstruct a significant corpus of terracottas of exceptional quality (see Gentilini 1992, pp. 371ff.; Bellandi 1998, pp. 282–85 and relevant catalogue entries). These terracottas include many close comparisons with the present sculpture. One such example is the Madonna and Saints in San Mauro in Signa (c. 1515), where we find the same type of angels, tonality of glazes (bright yellow, pale blue, brilliant green), extensive use of red pigment applied "a freddo", Sarto-like drapery, and melancholic expression. Other points of close comparison are the bust of the Savior in the Victoria and Albert Museum, which is similar in the complex and lively modeling of the hair, and the San Galgano in San Cristoforo in Siena, which is comparable in the depiction of profound expression. It is no exaggeration to say that, along with his brother Girolamo, Luca il Giovane was responsible for the continued flowering of the art of the Della Robbia in the sixteenth century.

Giancarlo Gentilini

GIAMBOLOGNA

Mercury

GIAMBOLOGNA
(Douai 1525/29–1608 Florence)

MERCURY
Bronze, 183 cm. (72 $\frac{1}{2}$ inches) in height,
c. 1600–1625

Provenance:
Private Collection, Florida
Private Collection, New York City

Relevant Bibliography:
C. Avery, *Giambologna*, Oxford, 1987, pp. 21–25,
37, 124–130, 250, 256.

Photographs before cleaning

fig. 1
Giambologna, *Mercury*
Museo Nazionale del
Bargello, Florence

The present statue is closely related to the *Medici Mercury* now in the Bargello (fig. 1). The extensive flawing of the bronze combined with the careful patching of its surface with threaded plugs suggests a cast of the earlier part of the 17th century, not far in date from the period of Giambologna's lifetime, when technical shortcomings were part and parcel of contemporary foundry technique, which was still run by rule of thumb, guesswork and—literally—prayer, rather than on purely scientific principles. Indeed, the *Medici Mercury* itself is a very flawed cast that has sprung apart along some of the fault-lines and has had to be repaired fundamentally in the 20th century. The surface of the present statue has been lovingly polished with abrasives (such as pumice powder) and the details have been minutely and painstakingly incised with the burin.

This is the only full size cast of the composition that can lay claim to an origin within the workshop system established by Giambologna. It may even have been cast from the same piece-moulds used to produce the *Medici Mercury* in 1580. These would have been carefully laid aside for future use and may have been employed to cast a statue ordered eighteen years later by King Henri IV (see below). The full size cast of Mercury that crowns the central fountain in the National Gallery of Art, Washington D.C., is currently considered to be a Roman cast of the late eighteenth century, while other reproductions have been produced throughout the nineteenth and twentieth centuries by commercial foundries in Naples and Florence.

fig. 2
Giambologna, *Mercury*
Museo Civico, Bologna,

Giambologna, as the Italians called the Flemish immigrant Jean Boulogne, settled in Florence soon after 1550 and became court sculptor to three successive Medici Grand-Dukes. Giambologna originally devised his Mercury in flight, a compositional *tour de force*, in 1563 to crown a column in the courtyard of the University at Bologna (lost, and its appearance is not recorded) where he was primarily engaged in creating his famous *Fountain of Neptune*. He was initially inspired by a bronze statuette of *Mercury* in one of the niches on the pedestal of Cellini's *Perseus and Medusa* (which had been unveiled in the Loggia dei Lanzi in Florence in 1554, just after he had himself arrived in the city). He set himself a task that was virtually impossible—and unsuitable to the heavy materials of sculpture—to represent a figure in flight. The ancient Roman poet Virgil envisaged Mercury, messenger of the gods and of Jupiter in particular, as "stirring up the winds and flying through the turbulent clouds", when he flew about the heavens on his errands (Virgil, *The Aeneid*, book IV, lines 245–46: *Agit ventos et turbida tranat nubila)*, and it is this sort of image that Giambologna sought to evoke.

From Michelangelo Giambologna had learned the importance of making preliminary models to explore a composition and this enabled him to create this vibrant sculpture. Starting as was his normal practice with a wire armature to support the daringly outflung limbs, he must have deftly built up the svelte nude form around it with pellets of wax, as in the surviving models in the Victoria & Albert Museum. The results are preserved in a bronze cast from such a model now in Bologna (fig. 2). The general lie of the limbs in a radial pattern was derived from a low relief

fig. 3
Giambologna, *Mercury*
Kunsthistorisches Museum,
Vienna

design on a medal of a few years earlier (c. 1551) by Leone Leoni showing Mercury hurtling through the clouds of heaven above a landscape. Giambologna's achievement was to render this complex design in full three-dimensional form and make it balance above the fulcrum of the ball of its left foot. The center of gravity of the torso had to be vertically above—with the limbs balanced evenly—to minimize lateral strain on the narrow ankle.

The composition in the model was evidently regarded as a success and the sculptor later refined its comparatively naturalistic and classical proportions in bronze statuettes of 1565 and 1579, now in the museums of Naples, Dresden and Vienna, into the elongated shaped beloved of Mannerism (fig. 3). The running motion was drawn vertically into a yet more balletic pose, exemplifying the aspirations of humankind to fly like a bird.

However, for a nearly life-size enlargement (approximately 180 cm. high) required by the Medici in 1580 to crown a fountain in front of the loggia of their villa in Rome (fig 1 and 4; the version now in the Bargello, Florence), Giambologna reverted to the more acceptably naturalistic proportions of his original design in Bologna. Presumably the scale would have made the more

fig. 4
G. F. Venturini,
*Fountain of Mercury in the
Garden of Villa Medici*
(detail)

artificial proportions of the intervening small bronze versions look more pronouncedly anomalous. A similar change had occurred when Cellini enlarged his models for the statue of *Perseus* to go in the Loggia dei Lanzi, for the finished figure looks far more solid. Specific preferences of his patron, Cardinal Ferdinando de'Medici, who was a great admirer of classical sculpture, may also have been taken into account.

A decade after he cast the statue for Villa Medici, Giambologna was called upon to provide a similar figure for King Henri IV of France, whose wife, Maria, was a Medici. The new statue was sent to France, along with another bronze for a fountain, a *Triton*, (now in the Metropolitan Museum of Art, New York) in 1598. A *Mercury* of a variant model from the gardens of St. Cloud (now in the Louvre) is normally identified with this documented piece, but its quality is not as high as one would have expected of a royal commission produced under the sculptor's direct supervision, nor is it equivalent to that of the *Triton*. The present, newly emerged, cast of the *Medici Mercury* is therefore a possible alternate candidate for the statue produced for Henri IV.

Giambologna's composition has proven to be immensely popular even until our own day. After being reproduced as a statuette throughout the seventeenth century, it was the only non-classical sculpture included in the list of Giacomo Zoffoli, the Roman bronze caster of the late eighteenth century, who catered to the English aristocracy on the Grand Tour: an early example was imported in England in 1763 by the Marquis of Tavistock (Woburn Abbey). Zoffany's portrait of the Dundas family shows Giambolgna's perfectly balanced figure being used as the centerpiece of a whole *garniture de cheminée*, consisting otherwise of reductions after celebrated classical bronzes. It was a signal honour for a 'modern' sculptor in those days to have his work considered on a par with those of the ancients. Usually only Michelangelo was accorded that distinction.

Charles Avery

NORTH ITALIAN SCULPTURE

MASTER OF TROGNANO
(BARTOLOMEO DA COMO?)

Madonna and Child with Two Angels

MASTER OF TROGNANO
(BARTOLOMEO DA COMO?)
(Lombard, late fifteenth century)

MADONNA AND CHILD
WITH TWO ANGELS
Polychromed wood (poplar), 69.5 x 47. 5 cm.
(27.5 x 18.5 in.), made c. 1490

Provenance:

Carlo de Carlo, Florence

Bibliography:

R. Casciaro, *La scultura lignea lombarda del Rinascimento*, Milan, 2000, pp. 84, 284–285, cat. 54.

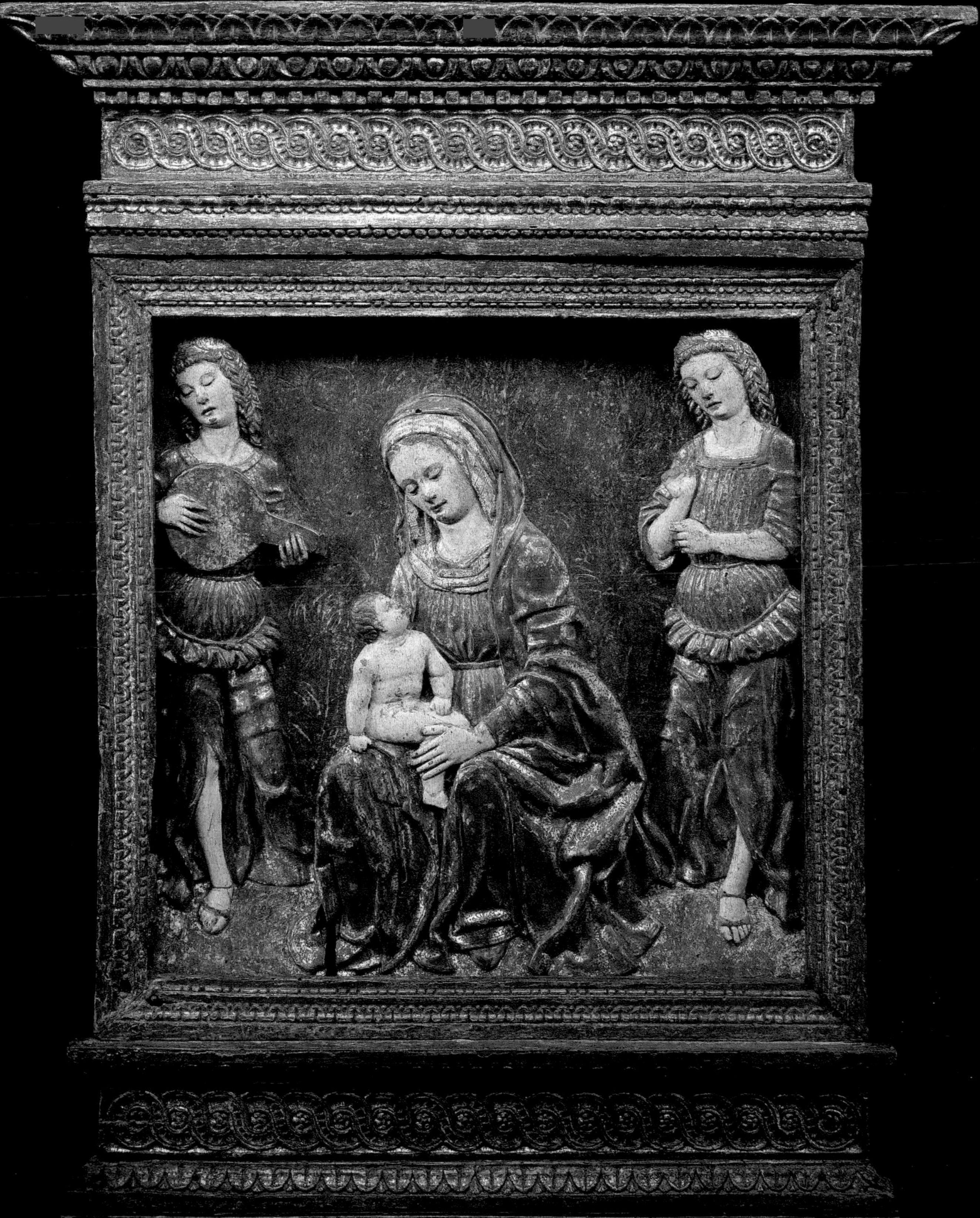

The *Madonna and Child with Two Angels* is an extremely rare masterpiece of Italian wood sculpture of the Renaissance. Of exquisite delicacy, especially in its depiction of gesture and expression, the piece is by the Master of Trognano, a Lombard artist of the late fifteenth-century, whose importance has recently been recognized. New evidence, to be discussed below, shows that the Master can perhaps be identified as Bartolomeo da Como.

We do not know the provenance of this sculpture, which in recent years has been in the collection of Carlo de Carlo in Florence. (An old Hahn Brothers label on its frame shows that it was in New York City sometime earlier in the twentieth century.) Enclosed within its beautiful and substantially complete original frame, the relief is extremely well preserved. Small losses are found in the fingers of the right hand of the angel at the right, and there is a break in the Virgin's robe at the lower left. The polychromy, which was executed for the most part over a layer of gold-leaf, is abraded and the red bole under the gilding shows through in many places. The skin-tones have survived better than the other pigments and are almost wholly intact, as is the veil around the Madonna's head, which displays a refined decoration in white picked out on the gilding.

The relief depicts a moment of affectionate intimacy between the Madonna and Child; they are accompanied by angel musicians, whose presence highlights the liturgical aspect of the scene. The angels seem to descend from analogous figures in paintings of the *Adoration of the Magi* or the *Nativity*, for example Piero della Francesco's picture in the National Gallery, London. As was typical in Renaissance art, the angels' features have an almost feminine beauty, and their clothes are generally based on both antique costume and contemporary fashion.

The Child is completely nude and His muscular body is reminiscent of images of the baby Hercules, perhaps in order to emphasize His earthly nature, in contradistinction to the heresies that attributed to Him a solely divine nature. With a powerful twist of the body, He turns toward the Madonna, who inclines her head toward Him, her eyes half-closed in a thoughtful and almost melancholic expression.

In style, the figures are closely related to the body of works that have been grouped together under the name, the "Master of Trognano," in reference to the known provenance of a splendid relief of the *Adoration of the Shepherds*, today in the Pinacoteca Malaspina in Pavia (fig. 1). My suggestion to identify the author of this relief with the artist of the scenes of the Passion that were originally in Santa Maria del Monte sopra Varese has been accepted by other scholars (e.g. M Binaghi Olivari, in *Il tesore dei poveri* ed. by M. Bescape, Milan, 2001.) The altar of that church was adorned with four reliefs of the Passion; two of these are now in the Museo del Castello Sforzesco in Milan, and the other two are now in the monastery of Romite Ambrosiane in Rome and cannot be viewed by the public. A fact that has recently come to light appears to confirm the connection between the two reliefs in Milan and the relief from Trognano. The two works in Milan had been removed from Varese and donated in 1689 to the parish of Bascapè, near Pavia.

fig. 1
Master of Trognano,
Adoration of the Shepherds
Pinacoteca Malaspina, Pavia

Trognano is also in the parish of Bascapè. Therefore, one is tempted to imagine that the relief of the *Adoration of the Shepherds*, formerly in Trognano, also came there from Santa Maria del Monte; it may even be included among the elements referred to in a contemporary document as "pluribus aliis brevioribus," which are no longer otherwise identifiable.

The ancient altar of Santa Maria del Monte was one of the principal commissions of the Sforza family during the years 1482–1491, and standing before it we find ourselves in front of a work and of an artist of the first rank. His identity is still a matter of debate, although new evidence may have finally solved the issue (see below). He was a woodcarver with a profound knowledge of Mantegna's prints, from which he even derived the compositions of several of his works. He was also familiar with the Prevedari print, based on a drawing by Bramante in 1481, which he cited in the architecture of the *Adoration of the Shepherds* from Trognano.

Many features of the present sculpture resemble those of the *Adoration of the Shepherds* from Trognano, and also those of the reliefs from Santa Maria del Monte. Note, for example, the foreshortened faces and bodies, sculpted in very low relief that nevertheless create a great sense of spatial relationships. Moreover, the features of the face are sweet and delicate, with the exception of the typical emphasis of the eye-lids, which are somewhat heavy and protuberant, as was typical in works by Lombard woodcarvers of the Quattrocento, but without any of those strong expressive underlinings so frequent in that region. The angels that accompany the present *Madonna and Child* are comparable in every detail with those of the *Adoration of the Magi* from Trognano; they are exactly alike in their drapery, anatomy and physiognomy.

The extremely fine quality of the carving—at the highest level of Lombard sculpture of the period—the care of the details, the exquisite precision in delineating the outlines of the figures, and the capacity to achieve both dramatic foreshortening and lively movement in very low relief demonstrate that the present work ranks among the very few works that can be securely attributed to the Master of Trognano.

The one possibility to identify the name of this master is presented by the documents for the work at Santa Maria del Monte. One certain record that concerns the wood sculptors active at the church is dated 11 June 1478 (published by R. Ganna, *Arte Lombarda*, 1996, pp 64–71). From this document we know that there were six artists active in carving the choir of the church: Giacomo Del Maino, Giovan Pietro De Donati, Bernardino Maggi, Ambrogio d'Angera, Bernardino Porro and Bartolomeo da Como. The analogies between the surviving sections of the choir and the reliefs formerly on the altar are so extraordinarily close that they provide a chance to identify the "Master of Trognano" among the six artists named in the document.

Giacomo Del Maino, the most famous of the group, shortly later made the altarpiece frame for San Francesco Grande in Milan, in which Leonardo da Vinci placed his painting of the *Madonna of the Rocks*. Thanks to recent research, Giacomo's style can now be identified, and it is both much more plastic and vigorous, and cruder and more archaizing than that of the present sculpture (see Casciano 2000, pp. 63–85, 272–281, 367–70).

Benardino Maggi is known to have prepared in 1487 a wood model of the *tiburio* of the Duomo of Milan, on the basis of Leonardo's drawing; unfortunately, the model no longer survives. As the model, indisputably, was more a piece of carpentry than of sculpture, one may hypothesize that his work in the choir of Santa Maria del Monte was of a structural nature, although more information is necessary in order to be certain.

Little is known about Bernardino Porro, beyond the facts that he was the "filius Jaonneti Fazini" [son of Giovanni Facino] and lived in Lentate near Milan. An artist with the same name is documented in the Certosa of Pavia in 1496 working with Tamagnino and Amadeo, but the documents state that artist's home was Bissone on the lake of Lugano. In any event, he does not seem to have been an artist of the first rank.

Ambrogio d' Angera is a well-known collaborator of Giacomo Del Maino. He can probably be identified as the author of the Madonna in the sanctuary at Intra, near Angera, the artist's home town; it is a sculpture very similar in style to that of Del Maino.

Giovan Pietro De Donati is the best documented of all these artists (see Casciano 2000, pp. 291–320). With his brother he was the author of an enormous quantity of statues and reliefs in wood for almost the entire Duchy of Milan. Their style is easily recognizable, and it presents some parallels with that of the Master of Trognano. But instead of the light grace of that artist, the works of De Donati are harder and more robust.

This leaves Bartolomeo da Como, "filius quondam domini Antoni civitati Mediolani porte Ticinenesis parochjie sancti Sebastiani" [son of the late Antonio, citizen of Milan, resident in the parish of St. Sebastian near the Ticino gate]. Up to now, no works by the artist have been identified, but his name appears in two documents. In one he appears as the witness to a pact between the artists Amadeo and Francesco Cazzaniga (30 June 1483); and in the other among the procurators "ad causas" named by Amadeo (28 November 1500). (For these documents, R. Schofield, J. Shell, G. Sironi, *Giovanni Antonio Amadeo. I documenti*, Como, 1989, doc. 87 and doc. 670.) It is not known if this connection with Amadeo indicates that Bartolomeo da Como also worked in marble. What is known is that, at least for the period from 1478 and 1500, he collaborated in some of the most prestigious workshops of the Duchy of Milan.

In her forthcoming study, Maria Teresa Binaghi Olivari accepts my hypothesis that the Master of Trognano is to be found among the artists named in the document of 1478; and she proposes, furthermore, that he is to be identified specifically with Bartolomeo da Como. In favor of this theory, she cites the connection of Bartolomeo with Amadeo and Cazzaniga, whose sculptures display evident affinities with the Master of Trognano's *Adoration of the Shepherds*. Particularly suggestive analogies appear in comparison with the reliefs of Cazzaniga and Benedetto Briosco for the tomb of Pier Francesco Visconti di Saliceto (1484), now in the National Gallery of Art and the Cleveland Museum of Art. Their architectural elements, passages of drapery and compositional solutions are generally similar. It should be noted that the quality of the relief from Trognano is indubitably superior to that of the reliefs of the Visconti tomb. Nevertheless, this is not to dispute Binaghi's conclusion that "it seems we should locate stylistically the *Adoration of the Shepherds* near the workshop of Cazzaniga and Briosco a little after 1484." Binaghi, however, also emphasizes that the similarities with the two marble artists are insufficient to explain the complexity and wealth of the Master of Trognano's visual culture. She notes the relationship of his works to Bramantino's paintings, in particular the *Philemon and Baucis* in Colonia, the *Madonna and Child* in Boston, the *Nativity* in the Ambrosiana, and the *Adoration of the Magi* in London. The Master's works also display his knowledge of Bramante's architecture.

There are only a handful of works which seem to evince the extremely refined style of the Master of Trognano. Among these the present work occupies a position closer to the *Adoration of the Magi* than to the reliefs of the Passion. The harsher and more archaistic elements of the Passion reliefs have been overcome in favor of a softer and more fluid composition. Thus, the date of the piece is likely to be around 1490–95.

Raffaele Casciaro

ANDREA MANTEGNA

Pietà with Angels

ANDREA MANTEGNA
(Isola di Carturo 1430/1–1506 Mantua)

PIETÀ WITH ANGELS
Polychromed wood, 73 x 52 cm. (28 $^3/_4$ x 20 $^1/_2$ in.),
made c. 1450

Provenance:
Private Collection, Paris

fig. 1
Donatello, *Dead Christ
Tended by Angels*, Victoria
and Albert Museum,
London

This extraordinary but unpublished sculpture represents the dead Christ supported on the edge
of his tomb by two young angels. Christ's face is slack in death, His eyes and lips partially open,
and His body is stiff and lifeless. The angel on the left throws his head back in anguish as he
reaches under Christ's right arm to delicately touch His cheek. The angel on the right lovingly
presses his face against Christ's shoulder as he grasps His left arm and torso. The angels' faces are
contorted with grief and bewilderment, and they both look up, as if looking to God the Father in
heaven, imploring Him for understanding. This interpretation of the sculpture possibly finds support in a hymn that was sung during Matins on Holy Saturday (between Good Friday and Easter
Sunday). It contained the words, "O Life, how can you die? how can you dwell in the tomb?…
The angelic hosts are at a loss to understand the mystery, O Christ, of your ineffable and inexpli-
cable burial" (quoted in R. Coffey, "The Man of Sorrows of Giovanni Bellini, Sources and
Significance," Ph.D. dissertation, University Madison-Wisconsin, 1987, p. 101). The grief-sticken
angels are part of the heavenly host unable to comprehend the death of Jesus.

Representations of this scene, generally known as the Pietà with Angels, were a popular subject in Renaissance art. But the specific gestures that the angels make in this sculpture—touching
or supporting His head, and pressing the face against His shoulder—are extremely rare in such
images. As has been shown by Andrea de' Marchi, this iconography was strongly associated with
the Veneto; indeed, almost all such images, where the original location is known, were made for
either Verona or Padua. The earliest extant example is a marble relief by Donatello (Victoria and
Albert Museum, London), which Pope-Hennessy believed was probably made in Padua around
1445 (fig. 1). Another early instance is a drawing from c. 1455–60 by Marco Zoppo, the Paduan
artist (fig. 2).

In style, the present sculpture is remarkably similar to that of another artist active in Padua
around 1450: Andrea Mantegna. Indeed, there are so many close points of comparison with his
works that the statue can be reasonably attributed to Mantegna himself. (There is literary and

fig. 2
Marco Zoppo,
Dead Christ with Angels,
British Museum, London.

documentary evidence that Mantegna was a sculptor as well as a painter, as will be discussed below.) The strength of the evidence can be demonstrated in a detail-for-detail comparison of the scupture with Mantegna's paintings. Every feature of the sculpture finds exact parallels with aspects of his other works.

Let us begin with the figure of Christ. He can be directly compared with the image of Jesus in the St. Luke altarpiece of 1453–1454 (fig 3). The heads are similar in shape, and the treatment of their details are highly alike. For example, in both figures the eyes are widely set in the sockets, and the crescent shape of the eye-lids is almost exactly the same. The mouths are also comparable. Both are open, revealing the teeth, and in shape the lips are nearly identical. The head of Christ in the sculpture can also be compared with the head of St. Luke in the altarpiece (fig. 4). Note, especially, the correspondances in the treatment of the wide-set and pointed cheekbones, and the similar treatment of the lines furrowed in the brow. Another point of comparison for the head of Christ is that of St. James in the fresco of *St. James on the Way to Execution*, in the Ovetari Chapel (fig. 5). The relation of the head of the body and the shape of the mouth are especially alike.

The form of Christ's beard is idiosyncratic and particular. On the chin, it divides into two symmetrical and helical locks. A close match for this feature appears in the beard of Christ in the Resurrection panel from the San Zeno altarpiece, and also in the drawing and prints of *Risen Christ between Saints Andrew and Longinus* (fig. 6). It is also like the beard of St. John the Baptist in the *San Zeno altarpiece*, and the beard of Christ in *Five Designs for a Cross*.

fig. 3
Andrea Mantegna, *Head of Christ*, detail from
St. Luke altarpiece

fig. 4
Andrea Mantegna, *Head of St, Luke*, detail from St. Luke
altarpiece, Brera, Milan

fig. 5
Andrea Mantegna, St. James, detail from *St. James on the Way to Execution*, Ovetari Chapel, Padua

fig. 6
Andrea Mantegna, *Risen Christ between Saints Andrew and Longinus*, (detail) Rijksprentenkabinet, Rijksmuseum, Amsterdam

Christ's body can be compared with depiction of his torso in a drawing of the Pietà from the 1460s (fig. 7). The arms hang away from the torso in a nearly identical fashion. This is especially evident when the drawing is seen in reverse (fig. 8). (This is not simply a matter of convention. For example, there is no painting by Giovanni Bellini of the Pietà where they hang exactly in this manner.) The arms of Christ in the sculpture can also be compared with the arms of the Virgin Mary in the *Crucifixion* panel from the *San Zeno altarpiece* (fig. 9). Furthermore, the treatment of Christ's hands is extremely similar to that of Mary's, although in reverse. (Compare Christ's right hand with Mary's left.) In the sculpture, the contour of Christ's hips and lower torso subtlely bulges outward in two shallow crescents at either side. A corresponding outline appears in the Pietà drawing. Note, too, that the structure of the torso in the sculpture resembles that of Christ in Mantegna's painting from c. 1500, *Pietà with Two Angels* (fig. 10). Both have broad, compact and high-set pectoral muscles, subtlely revealed rib-cages, and laterally creased abdomens.

The young angels provide additional evidence of Mantegna's authorship. Unmistakeably, they exhibit all the characteristics of Mantegna's distinctive type for baby heads. For example, they feature broad, almost pudgy, faces, narrow crescent-shaped eye-lids and open mouths that reveal the teeth. And as often in Mantegna's paintings, so here in the sculpture, the heads are shown at eccentric angles. Two close comparisons in Mantegna's paintings are the head of the infant Christ in the *Madonna and Child with Seraphim and Cherubim* from c. 1454 (fig. 11), and the head of the child in the *Madonna of the Caves* (fig. 12). Both of these heads are extremely similar to the head of the angel on the left; the shapes of the mouths, eyes and noses are especially alike. Some other relevant comparanda are the infants in the *Circumcision* (Galleria degli Uffizi, Florence), the seraphim and cherubim in the *Ascension* in the Ovetari chapel, and the angels in *Christ with the Virgin's Soul* (fig. 13). Indeed, the hair of the angels in this picture is divided into thick locks over the forehead, in much the same manner as in the sculpted angels. This feature of the sculpture is also found in some of the angels around the virgin in the Ovetari *Ascension* as well as in the angel with the column in the *Agony in the Garden* (National Gallery, London).

The angels in the sculpture have thick bands of fat on their legs: two bands on the thigh, and additional bands between the calf and the ankle. Mantegna regularly depicted the legs of children, putti and angels in this manner. Note, for instance, the legs of the infant in the *Madonna of the Caves* (fig. 12). Some other examples are the Christ child in the *Adoration of the Magi* (Galleria degli Uffizi, Florence), and the putti in the Camera degli Sposi.

The similarity of the sculpture to the work of Mantegna is not only in the details. It is also on the level of narrative imagination; specifically, the way in which the artist has used the interrelation of bodies and gestures in space to express emotion. One key to the power of the sculpture is the contrast of the motions of the heads of the three figures. This is especially true of the contrast between Christ and the angel to the left. The head of Christ falls forward and to the left, and

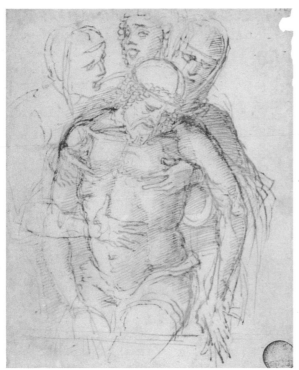

fig. 7
Andrea Mantegna, *Pietà*
Gallèria dell'Accademia, Venice

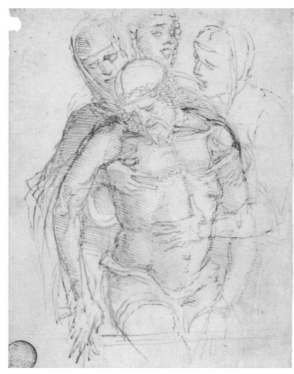

fig. 8
Andrea Mantegna, *Pietà* (shown in reverse)
Galleria dell'Accademia, Venice

fig. 9.
Andrea Mantegna, *Crucifixion panel from San Zeno altarpiece*
(detail), Musée du Louvre, Paris

fig. 10.
Andrea Mantegna, *Pietà with Two Angels* (detail)
Statens Museum for Kunst, Copenhagen

the head of the angel instead thrusts backward. An exact parallel for this is found in the group of the three Marys in the *Crucifixion* panel from the *San Zeno altarpiece* (fig. 9). There the Virgin's head falls forward and to the left and the head of the woman immediately behind her and to the right thrusts backward. The Pietà drawing (fig. 7) provides another parallel, as does the *Pietà with Two Angels* (fig. 10), where, again, you find the heads of Christ and an angel moving in opposite directions. In all these cases, this motif is used for the same effect: to highlight grief. To the best of my knowledge, this motif is unique to Mantegna. You do not, for example, find it in the Pietàs of Bellini or Zoppo.

Given the preponderance of the evidence, the case for the attribution of the sculpture to Mantegna is unusually strong and compelling. The majority of the close parallels for the sculpture date from c. 1450 to c.1460, and therefore the present work also appears to date at that time.

We should ask whether Mantegna actually carved the scultpure himself or whether he instead simply provided a drawing to an assistant and supervised his work. I believe the sculpture is autograph or essentially so. The quality of the details is exceptional. Consider, for example, the apparent delicacy with which the angel touches Christ's cheek; or the vivid contrast between the delicacy of this gesture and the violence with which the angel throws his head back in anguish. This degree of sensitivity in the description of spiritual and physical states is extraordinarily rare in Quattrocento sculpture. Moreover, the space between the heads of the angel and Christ seems to vibrate with emotional energy. Only a handful of the greatest artists of the early Renaissance were able to use the space between their figures as an integral part of their sculptures. The comparanda are Donatello's *Cavalcanti Annunciation* (Santa Croce, Florence), Luca della Robbia's *Visitation* (San Giovanni Fuorcivitas, Pistoia) and Andrea del Verrocchio's *Christ and St. Thomas* (Orsanmichele, Florence). It is hard to imagine more distinguished company.

There is literary and documentary evidence that Mantegna was a sculptor as well as a painter. Raphael's father, Giovanni Santi, wrote a *Cronaca* in verse during Mantegna's lifetime. In this text he recorded that Mantegna "has not omitted to work in relief in pleasing and graceful fashion, so as to show sculpture how much heaven and the sweet fates have bestowed upon him". In an epitaph for Mantegna written at the time of his death in 1506, Justus Caesar Scaliger praised him as a "pictor et plastes," that is, painter and sculptor. The Mantuan poet Fra Battista Spagnoli, writing c. 1490, said that Mantegna had surpassed not only the painters but also the scuptors of antiquity. "Why gaze on the statues of Myron and Lysippus? Why do the breathing marbles of Praxiteles and the statues of Euphranor delay your step? All the ivory of Phidias is overmatched. The genius of Polycletus is tarnished and loses all lustre when compared to the genius of Andrea." (All citations quoted from R. Lightbown, *Mantegna,* Berkeley, 1986, p. 130.)

A small number of sculpture projects by the artist are mentioned in documents and sources. In 1448 Mantegna was documented as one of the artists responsible for making the terracotta

fig. 11
Andrea Mantegna, *Madonna and Child with Serphim and Cherubim*, Metropolitan Museum of Art, New York

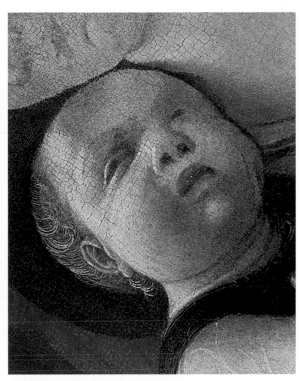

fig. 11a
Detail of fig. 11 rotated for comparison

fig. 12
Andrea Mantegna, *Madonna of the Caves* (detail)
Galleria degli Uffizi, Florence

fig. 13
Andrea Mantegna, *Christ with the Virgin's Soul*
Pinacoteca Nazionale, Ferrara

altarpiece of the Ovetari chapel. Scardeone, writing in 1560, stated that Mantegna cast his own bronze portrait, "sepultus est humi in phano divi Andreae, ubi aeneum capitis eius simulacrum visitur, quod suis sibi conflaverat manibus": 'he is buried in the church of Sant'Andrea, where the bronze portrait of his head can be seen, which he cast for himself with his own hands' (B. Scardeone, *De Antiquitate Urbis Patavii*, Basel, 1560, p. 372). In addition, Mantegna, at Isabella d' Este's request, designed a statue of Virgil (never erected), and he also made drawings for the tomb of Barbara of Bradenburg.

In the twentieth century, a handful of sculptures have been attributed to Mantegna. On the whole, these suggestions have not won support. However, two recent attributions deserve special recognition. Rodolfo Signorini and Anthony Radcliffe have published a small gilt bronze stauette of St. Sebastian, which they believe can be identified with a figure of Marsyas recorded in Isabella d'Este's studio (R. Signorini and A. Radcliffe, "'Una figura nuda legata a un tronco': una statuetta in bronzo dorato qui attribuita ad Andrea Mantegna," *Atti e memorie, Accademia nazionale virgiliana di scienze, lettere ed arti*, n.s. vol. LXV, 1999, pp. 48–104). Unmistakeably, the statuette is Mantegnesque in style, and the attribution appears to have received significant acceptance. Because it is a small and elegant work made approximately thirty or more years after the *Pietà with Angels* it has little bearing on this attribution. Clara Gelao has published a pair of polychromed marble statues of St. Eufemia and the Virgin Mary, now in the cathedral of Irsina (C. Gelao, "Per Andrea Mantegna: una precisazione e una proposta," in *Studi in onore di Michele D'Elia*, Matera-Spoleto, 1996, pp. 239–251). The figure of St. Eufemia is decidely Mantegnesque in style, and the attribution to the painter may be correct. (I have not seen the sculpture itself and the published photographs are too poor to be sure: you cannot see the details. For the same reason, its relation to the present sculpture cannot be determined.) The Virgin Mary, on the other hand, appears to be less Mantegnesque in style; but it is covered with modern paint making it especially hard to judge.)

It is possible that the *Pietà with Angels* was originally intended to serve as a private devotional image, much like the contemporary paintings of the same theme by Giovanni Bellini, Mantegna's brother-in-law. However, as Anthony Radcliffe has suggested to me, several factors suggest that the sculpture may have been intended to be placed in a lunette and to be seen from below. The tops of the heads of the figures are relatively unfinished, and the sculpture makes a powerful impression when viewed from a low viewing point. The general shape of the sculpture would also accomodate placement in a lunette. As the angels do not have wings, nor evident points of attachment for them, Radcliffe has also suggested that the wings may have been included in the background of the lunette in some fashion. (One frequently finds this arrangement in lunettes with angels by the Della Robbia.) Images of the Pietà often appeared in the central section of the upper tier of large polyptychs, both in sculpture and painting. The sculpture may have originally had a setting of this kind.

The condition of the *Pietà with Angels* is excellent with the exception of the evident losses of the right putto's foot and part of his arm, and the end of Christ's nose and the ends of several of his fingertips. The paint surface has evident abrasions and losses, but it is substantially integral, retaining most of its original highlights and details, and it is free of later overpaint. The gilding is original.

Andrew Butterfield

—

Contibutors

Charles Avery, formerly Deputy Keeper of the Department of Sculpture in the Victoria and Albert Museum, was from 1979 to 1990 Director of the Department of European Sculpture at Christie's. His books include *Florentine Renaissance Sculpture, Giambologna: The Complete Sculpture* and *Bernini, Genius of the Baroque.*

Alfredo Bellandi is an expert on Italian Renaissance Sculpture and the author of *Per un catalogo del Maestro delle Madonne in Marmo.*

Andrew Butterfield is Vice-President of Salander-O'Reilly Galleries and the author of more than sixty articles and books, including *The Collection of Victor and Sally Ganz, The Jacques Koerfer Collection, Early Renaissance Reliefs,* and *The Sculptures of Andrea del Verrocchio* for which he won the Eric Mitchell Prize.

Raffaele Casciaro is an expert on Italian Renaissance Sculpture; based in Milan, he has taught at the Università di Macerata and the Università di Lecce, and he is the author of *La scultura lombarda lignea del Rinascimento.*

A. Victor Coonin is Associate Professor of Art History at Rhodes College and the author of *The Sculptures of Desiderio da Settignano.*

Giancarlo Gentilini is Professor of the Storia dell'Arte Moderna at the Università di Perugia; he has published dozens of articles and books on Italian sculpture, including *I Della Robbia. La scultura invetriata nel Rinascimento* and *I Della Robbia e l'arte nuova della scultura invetriata.*

Anthony Radcliffe was from 1979 to 1989 Keeper of Sculpture at the Victoria and Albert Museum. He is the author of *European Bronze Statuettes,* and *The Robert H. Smith Collection. Bronzes 1500–1650* and co-author of *The Thyssen-Bornemisza Collection. Renaissance and Later Sculpture.* He was co-organizer of the international exhibition, *Giambologna* in 1978.

© 2001 Salander-O'Reilly Galleries, LLC
ISBN: 1-58821-102-9

Color Photography: Maggie Nimkin
Design: Martin Schott
Printing: The Studley Press